LOCKHARTS

Swap & Shop

This book belongs to

_____

Getting about in towns

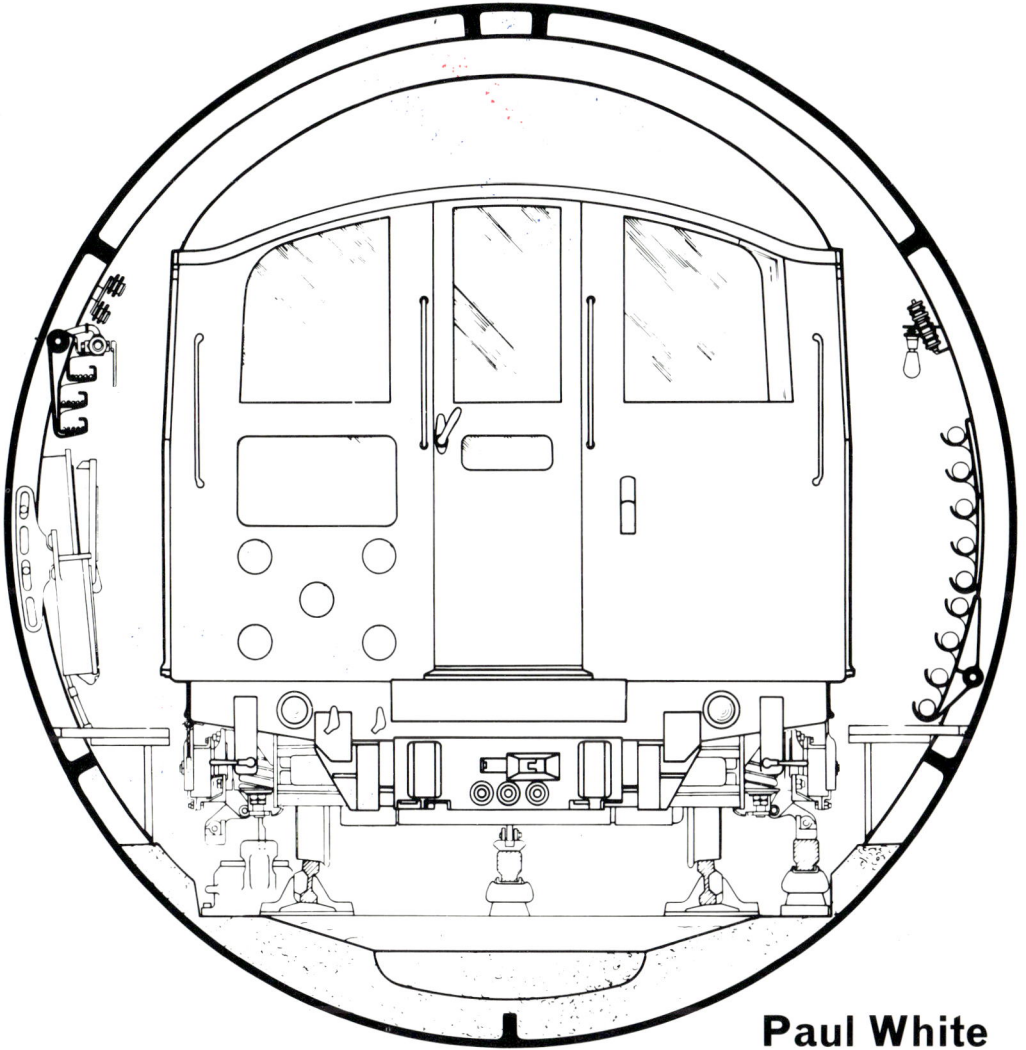

Paul White

Adam & Charles Black · London

Black's Junior Reference Books
General Editor R J Unstead

Chicago tram, 1893

British Library Cataloguing in Publication Data

White, Paul, 1944–
   Getting about in towns.—2nd ed.—
   (Black's junior reference books)
   1. Urban transportation—History—
   Juvenile literature
   I. Title
   388.4'09   HE305

   ISBN 0-7136-2593-7

Published by A & C Black (Publishers) Limited
35 Bedford Row, London WC1R 4JH

This edition published 1984
© 1984 A & C Black (Publishers) Limited
Earlier edition © A & C Black (Publishers) Ltd, 1976

ISBN 0-7136-2593-7

Printed in Great Britain by
BAS Printers Limited, Over Wallop, Hampshire

Melbourne bus, 1930s

Contents

Thomson's road steamer in
Edinburgh, 25 May 1870. It had rubber
tyres on the locomotive, and the
trailer had room for 65 passengers,
but it was too slow to be successful

Acknowledgements

The author and publishers are grateful to the following for permission
to reproduce illustrations:

Aerofilms Ltd 54c; Barnaby's Picture Library, 52a; W G Belsher 7b; British
Leyland 56b; British Rail, London Midland Region 25b; Chloride Technical
Ltd 57a; Express Dairies 57b; Tyne and Wear Transport 58a; Museum
of Transport, Glasgow 45b; Greater Glasgow Passenger Transport Executive 34c; Leeds City Council 38c, 54b; London Transport Executive, end-
paper, 1, 2b, 3, 5a, 14d & e, 19a, 20a & b, 21a, b, c, d & e, 24b, 25c, 27a
& c, 28b, 29a, 30a, c & d, 31b, 32c, 35c & d, 39a, 40a, b & d, 41b & c,
43b, 44, 45a & c, 46a, b, c, d & e, 47a & b, 48a, 49c, 50b, 51b & c, 55a
& b, 56a & c, 58b, 59, 62a, b & c; Mary Evans Picture Library 2a, 4, 7a,
10 & b, 13a & b, 14b & c, 15a, 17, 18a & b, 19b & c, 22b, 25a, 26a & b,
27b, 28a, 30b, 31a, 32a & b, 33b, 34a, 35, 36a, b & c, 37a & b, 40c, 42a &
b, 49a, 60, 63b; Mather & Platt Ltd 38a; Museum of London 10b; Radio
Times Hulton Picture Library 8, 9a & b, 11a & b, 12a, b & c, 16, 22a, 23,
24a, 26d, 29b, 33a, 38b, 39b, 41a, 43a, 49b & d, 50a, 52b; Science Museum
26c, 34b, 48b, 51a, 57c, 63a; South Wales Argus 61; M Szabo 37c & d;
US Information Service 53a; R J S Wiseman 58b.

Traffic in Dickens' London

1 Traffic in Towns

On the Tokyo underground during the rush hours, passengers are pushed into carriages so that the doors can be shut. In Los Angeles and Chicago, motorways in the centre of the city are sometimes jammed solid with cars, despite being many lanes wide. In London, nearly a quarter of the land surface is used for roads, yet the traffic crawls at a snail's pace and public transport (buses and railways) can scarcely cope with the huge numbers of daily travellers—the 'commuters'.

Traffic problems in cities are nothing new. Pepys's London and Dickens' London suffered chronic traffic jams. Even in ancient Rome, 2000 years ago, Julius Caesar had to ban wheeled traffic during the day. As a result the rumbling of wheels kept the citizens awake all night.

Hadrian, a later emperor, limited the number of carts which were allowed to enter Rome. This ban was later extended to all the towns of the Roman Empire—even those whose new wide streets had been planned for carts and chariots.

Traffic in London today

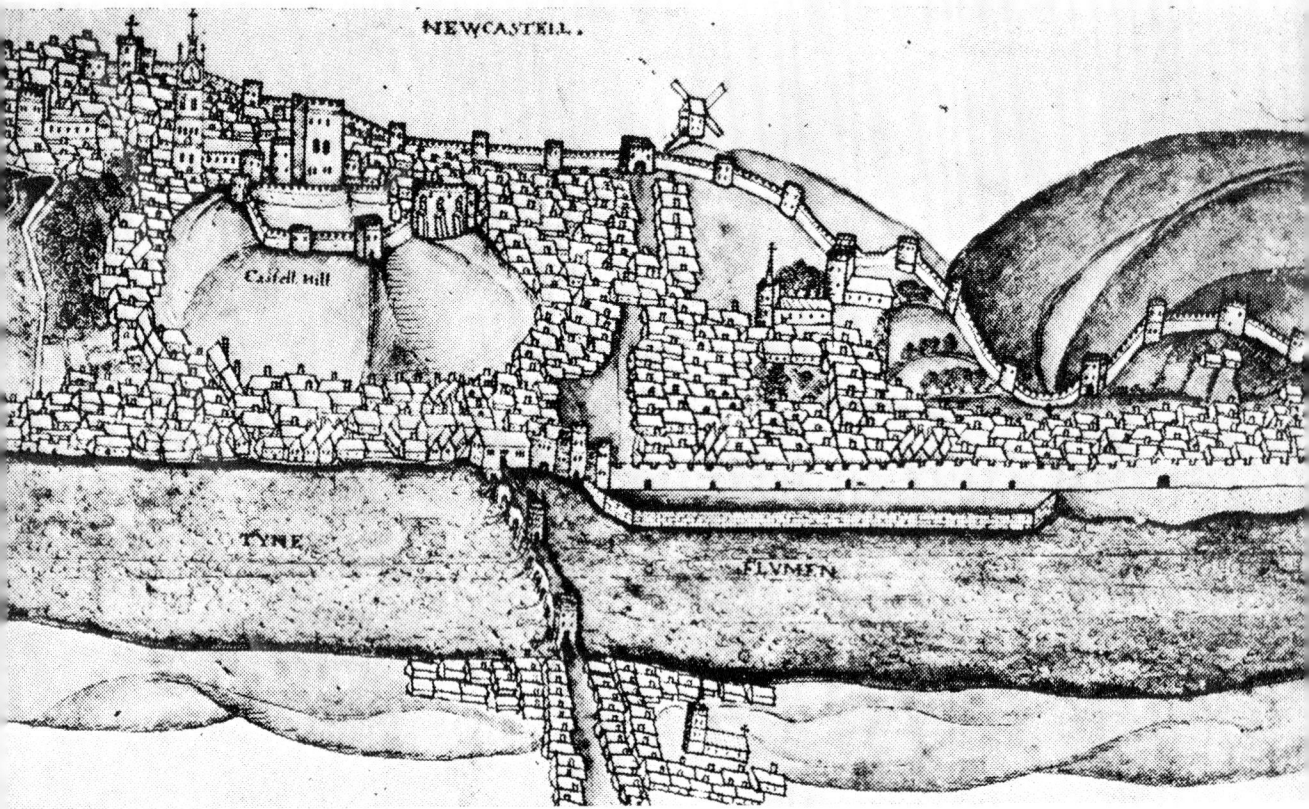

NEWCASTELL.

Castell Hill

TYNE

FLVMEN

Medieval Newcastle was small enough to walk across. Here we see the city from Gateshead, which was a 'faubourg' (see page 18), independent of Newcastle

2 The Medieval City

From the time of the Romans until the Middle Ages, few people in Europe lived in cities. The Saxons in Britain, the Franks in Germany and France, and the Norsemen of Scandinavia all preferred to live in hamlets or isolated farms. Their biggest towns were so small that we would call them villages.

After about AD 1000, towns grew larger and more important again. There was more trade, and weekly markets and yearly trade fairs were held in the towns. Some cities, such as Paris and London, attracted rich merchants from distant countries.

But even the largest of these cities was not too big to walk across, and most people, rich or poor, were prepared to walk. In any case, friends, churches, food-markets and jobs were always close at hand. People felt they belonged to a certain 'quarter' of the city. Many people worked downstairs in their own house, and lived in the rooms above.

Food came in daily from the farms around, carried in sacks on donkeys or in baskets on the heads of peasant women. In the great cities, merchants occasionally received trains of pack horses from distant lands, but this did not create much traffic. The merchants' quarter was often just inside the gate.

People had to pay taxes on everything they brought through the gates, whether it was fine armour from Milan, spices from the East or eggs from the neighbouring village. Friars were often prepared to hide a chicken or a goose under their robes and smuggle it past the customs officer at the gate.

Carts were used to carry dung out to the fields, and they returned with food, but there were no private carriages. Because there were few wheeled vehicles, there was no need for straight roads. Medieval cities were deliberately built with narrow winding streets, alleyways, small squares, enclosed courtyards and a few wider streets in which open-air markets could be held.

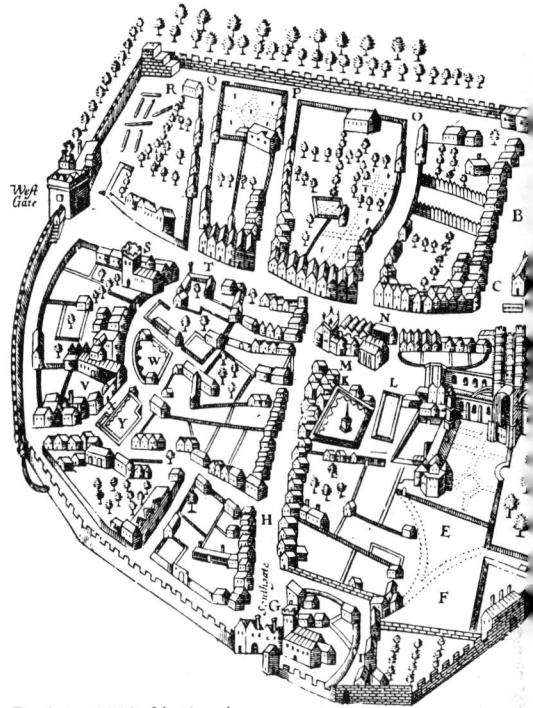

Bath in 1610. Notice how many gardens there are

Less than 100 years ago, pigs were still being driven to market in Digbeth, central Birmingham. The biggest changes in our cities have been very recent

Overhanging roofs protected the townspeople from sun and rain, and there were no 'wind-funnels' where a pedestrian could be blown off his feet on a gusty day. If the town was attacked, the attackers could not find their way about the maze of streets and alleyways, which gave the citizens more time to escape or organise a counter-attack.

In these narrow medieval streets, great merchants and poor apprentices jostled together. An arrogant noble-man might spread his feet wide in the stirrups, forcing people to take refuge in doorways on either side, but the man on foot found it easy to reach any part of the city.

The space saved by the narrowness of the streets was used for gardens, some of them large enough to grow vegetables or vines and all making the city more attractive to live in.

The open spaces in medieval towns, such as this vineyard, were built over in later centuries, so that more people could live within the walls. Overcrowding made squalid slums where there had been gardens

The French Court, like the English and Scottish, moved about the land on 'progresses'

3   The Capital City

The population of medieval London was about 40 000. By the 17th century it was 250 000 and growing fast. Yet at the same time other English cities were becoming rather less important.

Until James I's reign, the English Court moved about the country on 'progresses'. All the government officials moved with the king or queen, and so did all their files and records, carried in carts. By Stuart times, the records were becoming too bulky to move, and the officials too many. Government had to settle somewhere. Westminster, just outside the great trading centre of London, was a natural site.

As time went on, the king, courtiers, parliament and government officials (the 'Civil Service') spent more and more time in London. So did their servants, as well as the craftsmen and shopkeepers whose livelihood depended on wealthy men.

Fenchurch Street, London, in 1751

London's streets were still narrow, suited to pedestrians and horsemen. Coaches became quite common in Stuart times and traffic jams soon followed, especially when Parliament was sitting. Samuel Pepys complained in 1661:

'So to dinner at my Lord Crew's by coach, and in my way had a stop of above an hour and a half, which is a great trouble this Parliament-time, but it cannot be helped.'

and again:

'In King Street, there being a great stop of coaches, there was a falling out between a drayman and my Lord Chesterfield's coachman, and one of his footmen killed.'

away for hamerſmith

This couple are taking a boat to begin an evening out. A similar couple now might take a taxi

Londoners often used the Thames instead of the streets. Wherries could be hired at various 'stairs' along the river and many rich men had their own private boats.

As London grew beyond the walls of the medieval city, it spread along the crowded river, long and thin. From the pleasant village of Chelsea, through the Court at Westminster, past the palaces of the nobility along the Strand, through the City with its single bridge (always hazardous for small boats) and on beside the wharves of the greatest port in the kingdom, swept a constant stream of boats.

Downriver, the villages of Wapping, Rotherhithe, Deptford and Greenwich, with their shipyards, rope-walks and timber yards, were already almost a part of London, linked to the city by water.

The long thread of river was the main highway of Stuart London

LONDON

A coach-maker's shop

4 Some Town Vehicles

When Daniel Defoe visited Bristol about 1720, he reported:

'They draw all their heavy goods here on sledges without wheels, which kills a multitude of horses; and the pavement is worn so smooth by them that in wet weather the streets are very slippery and in frosty weather 'tis dangerous walking.'

In other cities, such sledges were not common, nor were slippery pavements. Not all the streets were paved or cobbled. In winter, country carts and lumbering wagons could become stuck in the filthy black mud.

Sledges in Madeira, about 1900. Perhaps the Bristol sledges were like this, though carrying goods, not people

In dry weather the surface of town streets was still rough, with ruts and potholes gouged out in winter. Coaches sometimes overturned, but more often broke their wheels or leather springs with the constant jolting. People accepted this as natural, and wheelwrights provided a rapid breakdown service.

The coaches never travelled much above walking pace. No-one used them for speedy movement, but to keep their fine clothes clean—and, of course, to show their high status in the world.

A sedan chair

'Rickshaw' sedans, like this, were popular for a while around 1700

Sedan chairs

Those who did not own a coach could hire a hackney coach or a sedan chair. Sedan chairs were introduced into England about 1620 by the Duke of Buckingham. His first sedan chair was carried high on the shoulders of the chairmen. The Duke was disliked by nearly everyone except the King, and this chair above the heads of ordinary mortals was detested by the people.

After Buckingham was assassinated in 1628, sedans were available for hire. They were carried at a lower level and were popular, more with ladies than with men, until the eighteenth century.

Coach and early sedan chair—this print is dated 1636

Hackney coaches

These could be hired in London from about 1600 until about 1910. They were not supposed to tour the streets looking for customers, which is called 'plying for hire', but in fact they often did. Although 300 to 400 were licensed at a time, there were always more to be found.

Fares in Stuart times were fixed at eightpence a mile, but the coachmen were notorious for cheating, for over-charging, and for their foul language to any customer who argued about the fare.

The hackney coach was not a specially built vehicle, but a private carriage no longer grand enough for its original owner. It was not smart. As the *London Magazine* said in 1825:

'Who can be a gentlemen and visit in a hackney coach? . . . wet straw and broken windows, and cushions on which the last dandy has cleaned his shoes, and stinking of the last fever it has carried to Guy's [Hospital] or the last load of convicts transported to the hulks [prison ships]'.

Since there were no special ambulances, hackney coaches were used instead. During the Plague of 1665, there was a law that a coach which carried a plague victim had to be aired and not used for five days.

Hackney cab about 1860 with a newly invented distance-gauge, or 'taximeter'. The cabbies refused to drive cabs with this invention. The taximeter was not used until motor-cabs were introduced (about 1908)—and the motor-cabs became known as 'taxis'

Coach springs sometimes broke, causing the horses to fall

Early cabriolet. This type was sometimes called a 'coffin cab'

Even the hansom cab was not quite safe. See page 63 for Joseph Hansom's original design

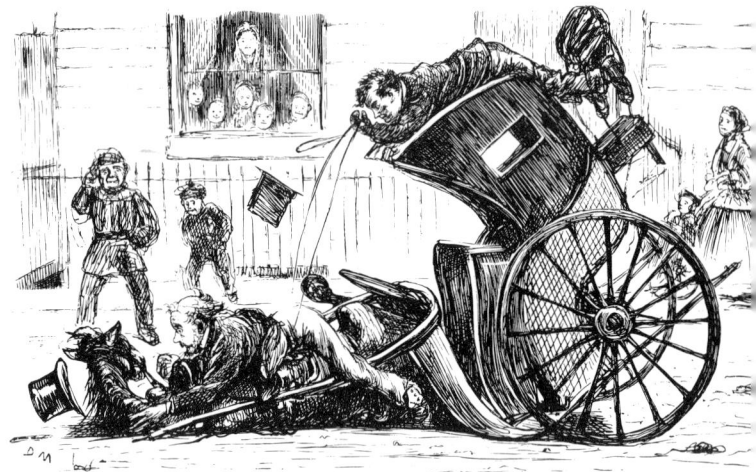

A two-wheel hansom, seating four, with the driver at the back

Cabs

From about 1800, Londoners could take a *cabriolet* ('cab') instead of a hackney coach. At first the cabs took only one passenger. They were faster than coaches, but if the horse stumbled, the passenger was thrown out head first.

Joseph Aloysius Hansom invented his first cab in 1834 in an attempt to increase safety. The famous *hansom cab* was in fact invented by John Chapman, though Hansom took the credit and gave it his name. Chapman seated the driver behind the passenger, improving the balance and taking the strain off the horse.

Other vehicles plying for hire in Victorian cities included the *growler*, a four-wheel cab seating two inside and a third beside the driver, the *tribus* with a door at the rear for its three passengers, and the *parlour hansom*, invented by Joseph Parlour in 1887. This was a four-wheeler seating four passengers, with the driver right at the back. By 1903 there were 7500 hansoms and 3900 four-wheelers in London alone.

Two views of the three-seater tribus

5 The Growing Cities

Streets fit for carriages

The rich men who owned coaches, and the well-to-do who hired them, complained about the winding narrow streets of the old cities. They wanted broad avenues designed for carriages, just as modern motorists now want inner-city motorways.

Because it was the rich and powerful who complained, the broader streets were often built. This happened at different times in the history of each city. It was not easy to get everyone to agree to rebuild an old town with a new street plan.

London was partly re-planned after the Great Fire in 1666. Sir Christopher Wren made a grand plan for the city, with broad ways between great squares and piazzas. Wren's idea would have made London grander and more impressive for visitors, but a less attractive place to live and work.

Part of the City of London, about 1680

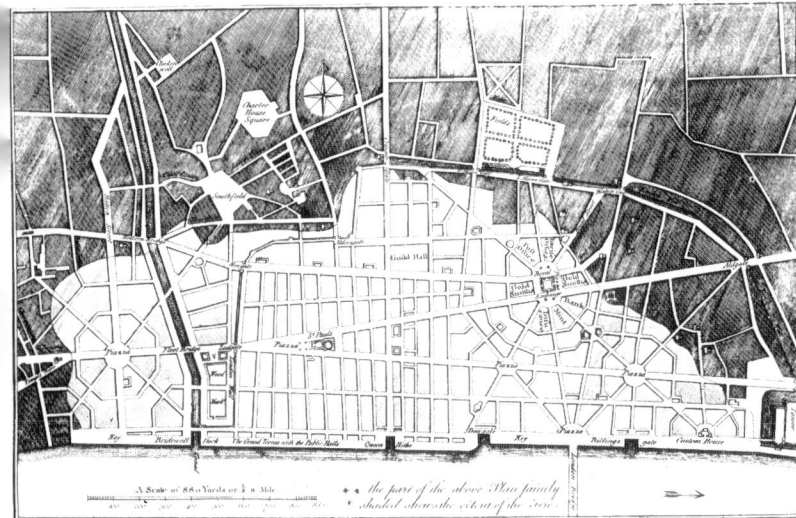

Wren's plan for rebuilding London

Luckily the citizens of London did not use Wren's plan. They rebuilt their city almost on the old street plan, and it survived until this century as a place for people on foot, living and working there, rather than a sight to be seen from a carriage.

Devonshire Square, about 1740. The carriage has come into the square through a tunnel-like passage, and the coachman waits in the square until the owner needs the carriage again

While the City remained a place for businessmen to meet in public places—at coffee houses, on the Exchange or walking about the streets—another part of London was developed specially for the aristocracy and gentry. This was the West End.

From 1660 onwards, new estates were built in the countryside west of the city—first Soho, then Piccadilly and Mayfair, and by the 1800s Belgravia and Kensington.

These estates were designed for people who used their carriages even to visit a near neighbour. Their large houses often faced onto a square. These squares now contain gardens, but originally some of them were parking places for visiting carriages. At the back of the terrace of houses was a 'mews'—a row of coach houses and stables, with rooms over them for coachmen and grooms.

The big houses needed local tradesmen, as well as servants. There had to be cobblers, laundresses and coal merchants within walking distance, so each fashionable area had small houses as well as grand ones. As yet there was no public transport, so all working people had to walk to their place of work.

The demand for suburbs

By the beginning of Queen Victoria's reign in 1837, the great industrial cities were growing faster than ever before. No longer was London the only large city in Britain. In Birmingham, Manchester, Glasgow and Liverpool, new factories employed more workers each year. The city populations increased dramatically.

Countrymen and their families moved to the towns, to live in cheap terrace housing. As the towns grew, those who could not find lodging near their work had to walk longer and longer distances to and fro.

The towns became fouler with smoke and bad smells, the din of machinery, the dirt, dust and ugliness of industry, and the risk of cholera and typhoid because of overcrowding and bad water supplies. People longed for the chance to live in the country, but they could not walk that far each day.

Scenes like this were becoming common in industrial cities. No wonder that people moved out to the suburbs if they could afford it

Suburbs were not a new invention. One kind of suburb, usually called by the French word *faubourg*, grew up outside the gates of medieval cities. Good examples are Southwark, across the Thames from London, and Gateshead, across the Tyne from Newcastle.

Faubourg traders were not members of the city gilds, and could undercut the city prices. Faubourgs also attracted entertainments which were forbidden in the city, such as Southwark's theatres and bath-houses.

In Queen Victoria's reign suburbs were built for the first time for the middle classes and even sometimes for artisans (skilled craftsmen). These people had their house in the suburb, but went to work each day in the city. The life of a Victorian suburb is beautifully described in *The Diary of a Nobody* (see page 63), which is set in Holloway, forty minutes walk north of the City of London. Forty minutes is a long walk on a wet night.

As people lived further out, they needed transport. Between 1834 and 1874, the number of private carriages in London rose from 100 000 to 400 000. But most people could still not afford to keep a carriage and horses. The first *public* transport service was the bus.

The idea for bus services came from Paris. This three-wheeler bus was operating there before 1830

This cartoon of 1829 shows 'the march of bricks and mortar' as new streets are built on the edge of London

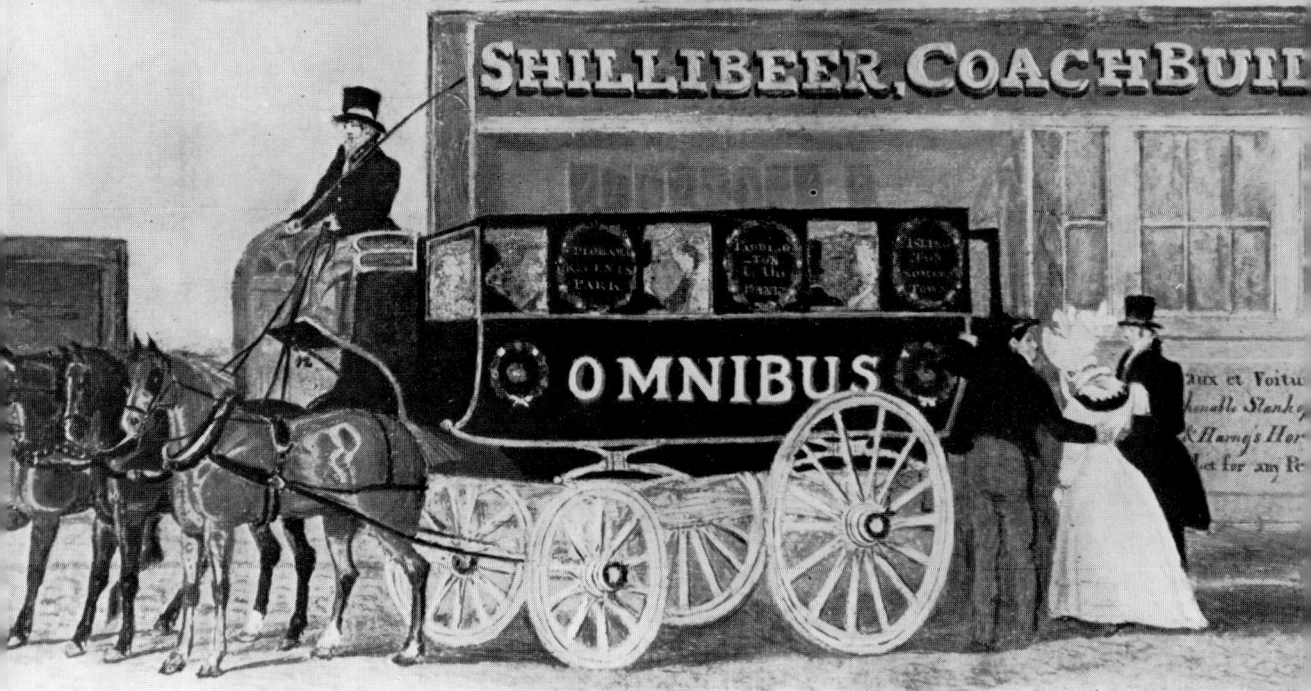

Shillibeer's omnibus

6 Horse Buses and Horse Trams

Horse buses

'Around the commercial quarter of Manchester there is a belt of built-up areas on the average one and a half miles in width, which is occupied entirely by working-class dwellings. Beyond lie the districts inhabited by the middle classes and the upper classes. The former are to be found in regularly laid out streets near the working-class districts ... The upper classes enjoy healthy country air and live in luxurious and comfortable dwellings which are linked to the centre of Manchester by omnibuses which run every fifteen or thirty minutes.'

Manchester omnibus, 1856

That was written in 1844. It is hard now to think of buses as upper-class transport, but bus fares at that time were very high.

The first bus service had been in Paris in 1662, but it failed and the idea was not re-introduced until about 1812 in Bordeaux, and again in Paris in 1828, when Stanislas Baudry ran 18-seater horse buses on several routes.

By 1836, steam buses were operating, but they were not a success

Baudry ordered some of his vehicles from an English coachbuilder, George Shillibeer, who thought it was such a good idea that he set up as a bus operator in London. His service started on 4 July 1829, between Paddington and the Bank.

Before the 'knifeboard' seat was invented, roof passengers sat on a single bench with their feet dangling over the side. Tall men sometimes broke the side windows with their heels

Shillibeer had two buses, each pulled by three horses, and carrying up to 22 passengers inside. The buses were clean and comfortable, the conductors were sober and polite, and newspapers were lent to the passengers on the way. The buses were immediately successful with well-to-do customers. The fare was one shilling from Paddington to the Bank—expensive in those days.

Shillibeer soon found his conductors were cheating him, as they had no ticket machines. He fitted an ingenious step, which counted the number of passengers who trod on it—but two conductors who were found cheating attacked the buses and beat up the inventor of the step.

There was trouble from the police too, who thought Shillibeer's buses were too big for London streets. So new buses were built, carrying only 16 passengers. That reduced the profit, because each bus collected fewer fares but still needed the same size crew and cost the same to run.

Eventually a 'knifeboard seat' was used on the roof, with passengers sitting back to back. Women could not climb up to the roof because of their long skirts, until in 1881 a curving staircase at the back replaced the simple ladder.

A long cord ran from end to end of the bus and was tied to the driver's left elbow. The driver stopped when the cord was pulled. Some drivers had a cord on each arm and were prepared to stop either side of the road, depending on which was pulled.

An 'improved omnibus' of 1847, with knifeboard. Notice how hard it was to climb up to the roof

Horse bus stables. By 1900 there were 40 000 horses in London to pull the buses

A bus from the Thomas Tilling fleet, 1864

French double-decker

Twenty-five years after the first 'shillibeers', there were 1000 buses in London alone, and 4000 by 1900.

Shillibeer himself soon sold his Paddington–Bank service, failed with a long–distance service to Greenwich (which competed with the faster and cheaper railway) and then succeeded as an undertaker. He invented a new kind of hearse, which in its turn was called a 'shillibeer'.

About 1900. Notice the curving staircase

Bus with a canvas awning against rain

New York in the 1850s

Train's tram at Birkenhead, 1860

Horse trams

Horse bus fares were never cheap. Really cheap travel—cheaper than anything before or since—came with the development of the tram.

The tram wheels moved so smoothly on their track that a tram horse could pull more weight than a bus horse and lived longer. For every £100 the bus companies spent on horses, the tram companies spent only £50, plus an extra £15 on maintaining the track.

Tram fares were much cheaper than bus fares, but because the demand for public transport grew faster and faster, tram systems and buses flourished together during the Victorian period. Both trams and buses were run by private companies.

These companies did not just serve existing areas. They made new routes into the countryside. Once land was linked to the town by public transport, people wanted to live there, so its value rose. Some transport companies bought land cheaply and then provided transport to it. Their buses or trams could afford to make a loss, because the company was making large profits from selling its land at increased prices.

Horse trams in Manchester's Piccadilly

The first public street tramway was probably one opened in Baltimore, USA, in the 1820s. New York had one by 1832. This had been planned as a steam railway, but the city sensibly refused to allow steam locomotives in its streets, so it was horsedrawn. American cities had even worse made streets than European cities, so trams were preferred to buses.

Britain's first street tramway ran in the Liverpool dock area in 1859, but lasted less than a year. In Birkenhead in 1860, George Train started a more successful tramway, though it used L-shaped rails which stuck up above the road. Train also laid trial lines in London, but they soon had to be relaid with the rails in grooves.

Before long there were hundreds of horse-drawn tramway systems in towns and cities throughout Britain and Ireland, and they quickly became thought of as a working-class transport system, particularly in London where they were kept out of the West End and the City itself.

Traffic jam in Victorian London

Increasing traffic

The streets were becoming more crowded. Buses and trams, drays, waggons, private and hackney carriages, and hansom cabs were all increasing in number. As the traffic grew thicker, vehicles had to stop and start far more often. Starting and stopping put a great strain on the horses. In 1840 bus horses worked for seven years: by 1890 they were worn out after four years.

A horse could not work all day. Ten horses (more in hilly districts) were needed to keep one bus working, so by 1900 there were 40 000 horses in London pulling the buses alone. No wonder the streets stank with horse droppings; dung flies and stable flies were everywhere.

But by 1914 there was not one horse bus or horse tram in London, and very few in the other major cities of Britain. They had been replaced by two new inventions—electric tramways and motor buses. You can read about these in chapter 8.

Breaking up a horse bus. This photograph is dated May 1911

'Let as fast as built'—a new suburb in 1901

7 Railways and the 'Underground'

Horsedrawn buses and trams travelled so slowly that a man could not live more than 6–8 km from his work.

Long-distance commuting only became possible with the growth of the railways. The first railways were built for inter-city travel and there were few suburban stations. Later, people who owned land near the main lines persuaded the railway companies to open extra stations.

At Ilford, for example, Archibald Corbett built 3000 houses and bargained with the railway company. If they opened a station, he would guarantee them £10 000 in season tickets over five years. Seven Kings station opened and was such a success that 15 trains left for the City between 8.30 a.m. and 9.30 a.m., and two more tracks had to be laid to cope with them.

Corbett's Ilford estates had unpaved roads, dusty in summer, quagmires in winter. There were no refuse collections, no entertainments, no churches. But he understood that the first thing a suburban commuter looks for when he buys a house is an easy journey to work.

In 1907 this station was in the country. Today it is a suburb

Commuters and train crew

New railways cut great swathes through cities and suburban villages, as these three pictures show

The Grand Central Station at Birmingham was opened 1 June 1854

Most railway passengers wanted to get right into the heart of cities. The early railway termini had often been built at the outskirts of the city, because the railway companies could not afford the price of land in the centre. The nearer they came to the centre, the dearer the land.

The companies were prepared to be ruthless, if they could afford it. Here is a report from the *Glasgow Citizen*, 1845:

'The proposal to blot out our ancient University and erect a grand railway terminus in its stead, has a boldness about it that is apt to upset minds of ordinary calibre. It is characteristic of the irreverent audacity of the railway system. Whatever comes in its way will inevitably be crushed or trampled down.'

That attempt did not succeed, but the railways often did cut broad routes through poorer areas, especially through the many frightful slums of Victorian cities. This was called 'ventilating' a city and was supposed to be a good thing. It was good to remove the slums, but the companies did not rehouse the people whose homes were destroyed, though of course they paid compensation to the landlords.

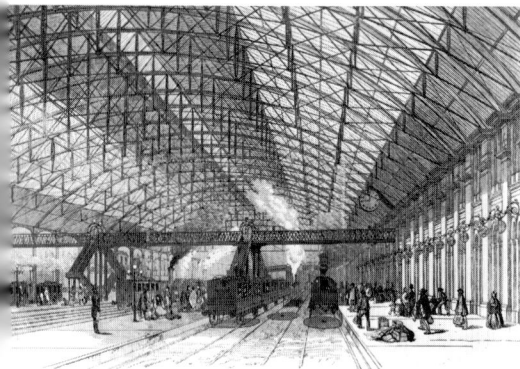

Narrow gauge train at Farringdon Road Station, 1866

The first underground

In Victorian London, an acre of land in the centre cost more than an acre anywhere else in the world. The railway companies would have liked to join all their lines at a great central station in the City, but none of them could afford the land on the surface.

So instead, the Great Northern and the Great Western Railway Companies decided to build a railway in a tunnel—an extraordinary decision at a time when all trains were pulled by smoky steam locomotives and many of the carriages were open like goods wagons.

This very first 'underground' was London's Metropolitan Line. It opened in 1863, connecting the termini at Paddington (Great Western) and King's Cross (Great Northern) with the City at Farringdon Road Station. Main line trains could run down to the Metropolitan Line, and at King's Cross they still did until 1976.

Since Paddington was a broad-gauge station, using 7 ft gauge instead of 4 ft $8\frac{1}{2}$ in, the whole Metropolitan Line had to be double-tracked. Some of the trains were broad-gauge and some narrow-gauge.

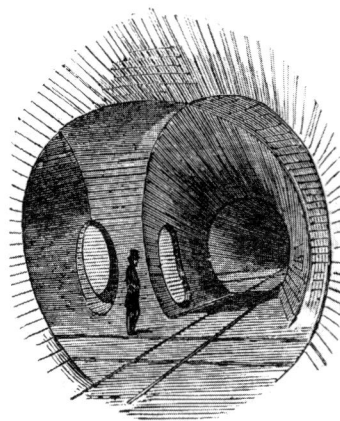

Signalmen stood beside the track with lamps and flags

Broad gauge train, 1863

KING'S CROSS. INTERIOR

King's Cross underground station, 1862

District Railway 4-4-0 tank engine with condensers (they look like drainpipes). The tiny carriages seated 80 first class, or 140 second class, or an astonishing 180 third class passengers

As many as six independent companies ran trains on the new railway, so their locomotives and carriages varied a lot, both in colour and design. All the locomotives were steam engines. They were specially adapted to condense their own steam, rather than exhausting it through the funnel. Even so, they made the air in the tunnels foul.

The special condensers made the engines cleaner but less powerful. If the train had to climb a gradient, the driver could give himself more power by exhausting dirty steam through the funnel—but the driver had no cab, so he had every reason to keep the exhaust clean!

By 1880 the 'underground' system had grown to include several lines into the suburbs, and the whole of the present Circle Line. Up to 20 trains an hour ran each way. The District Railway ran the clockwise trains and the Metropolitan ran the anticlockwise.

A journalist who rode on the locomotive of an anticlockwise train in the 1890s, described it like this:

'No time is wasted at stations on the Underground, and a minute later the train was off—off into a black wall ahead with the shrieking of ten thousand demons rising above the thunder of the wheels. The sensation was much like the inhalation of gas preparatory to having a tooth drawn. Visions of accidents, collisions and crumbling tunnels floated through my mind; a fierce wind took away my breath and innumerable blacks filled my eyes. I crouched low and held on like grim death.

Driver, stoker, inspector and engine—all had vanished. Before and behind and on either side was blackness, heavy, dense and impenetrable.'

Metropolitan Railway 4-4-0 tank

Blackfriars Station on the District Railway, 1875. The stations were mainly in cuttings, though the line between stations ran in a tunnel

The devastating effects of 'cut-and-cover' tunnelling

Tunnelling

The early underground lines were built close under the surface by the 'cut-and-cover' method. This was cheap, but as you can see from the pictures, nothing can happen on the surface while the work is being done. Traffic has to be diverted, perhaps for five years or more.

The route chosen for a cut-and-cover line has to be along a road, otherwise buildings have to be knocked down, or supported from below at great cost.

Under the surface of any city street there are pipes and cables—storm-water drains, sewers, gas, drinking water and nowadays telephone wires and electric cables. All these have to be found and moved without damaging them. When the Metropolitan line was being built, the Fleet Ditch sewer burst, and flooded a mile of the tunnels.

Photographs of the work in progress, 1861

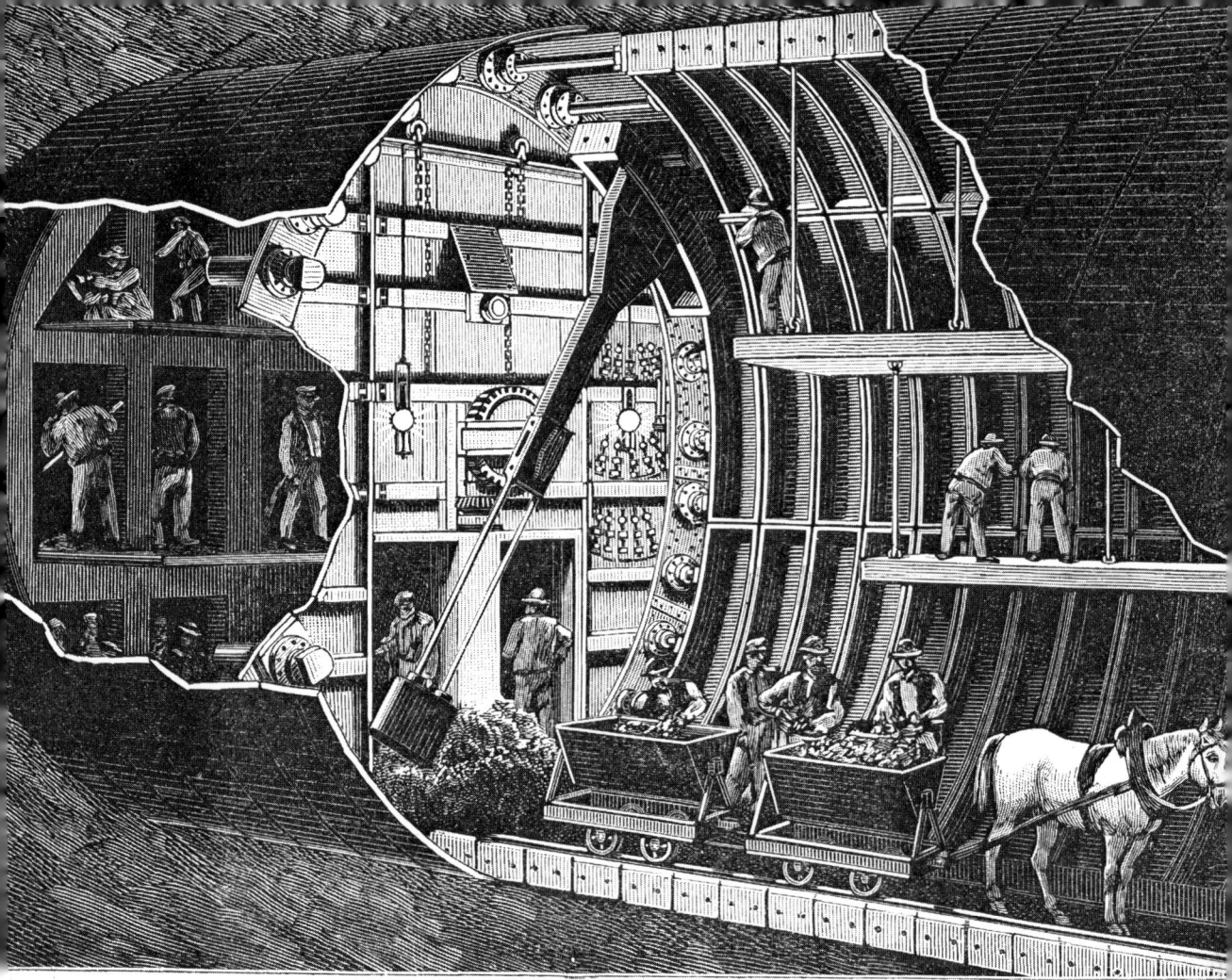

Shield tunnelling in progress, 1890

To avoid the pipes and cables, or to make a route that did not follow existing streets, it was necessary to tunnel much deeper. This was made easier by the invention in 1880 of the 'Greathead shield'. James Greathead's invention is still used for tunnelling today, though it has been improved.

The first deep-level or 'tube' railway was the City & South London Railway, opened in 1890 from the City to Stockwell. It is now part of the Northern Line, City branch.

Steam trains could not be used in a 'tube', and the City & South London planned to use cable haulage (see page 34). But the directors boldly decided to use electricity instead. So the first deep-level railway in the world was also the first British electric railway.

J C Greathead

The City & South London Railway

Dumpy little locomotives (which were soon found to be underpowered) pulled windowless carriages nicknamed 'padded cells'. 'The drain' was an instant success, carrying 15 000 passengers a day. It quickly had to be extended both north and south.

Each three coach train needed a crew of four – a motorman, his mate who did the coupling and uncoupling at the terminus, and two conductors. They looked after the folding entrance gates, which were on platforms between the carriages. There were only two exits for nearly 200 passengers on a full train.

Nonetheless, these 'padded cell' coaches were a big departure from the standard carriage designs still used at that time on the other underground lines, and were the ancestors of more modern designs on London Transport and other underground railways.

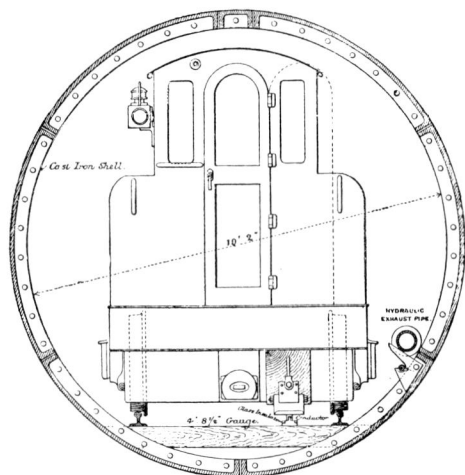

How the train fitted its 'tube' tunnel

Tunnelling work on the City & South London Railway

An alternative—the elevated railway

In some cities—New York, Berlin and Chicago for example—railways were built on stilts. Girder structures carried the elevated railway along the avenues of New York from 1868 onward.

Many cities had systems combining underground and elevated railways, for example Paris and Vienna. In Britain, elevated city sections of main-line railways were often built on viaducts. The railway company rented out the arches beneath as warehouse space or for small factories, and bridges carried the railway across the existing roads and streets.

Liverpool's elevated railway in the 1890s. It used electric power

New York elevated, 1879. The smoke from the steam locomotives made everything filthy

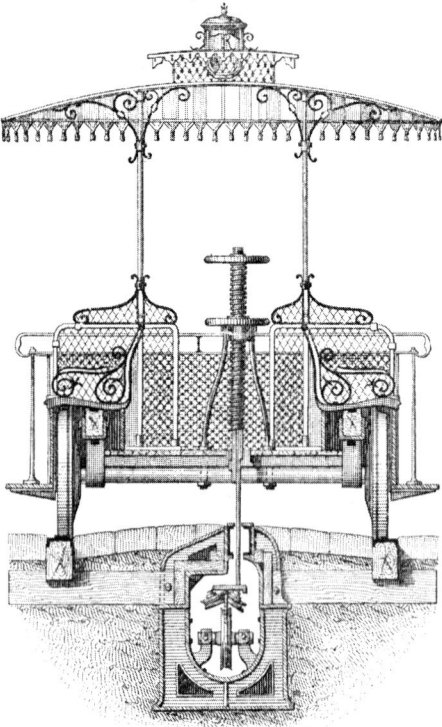

The cable-grippers on San Francisco trams worked like this

Glasgow

In the 1890s, an underground system was built in Glasgow which had neither steam nor electric locomotives. It used cable haulage.

Two endless cables went right round the 10·5 km circuit, one moving in each direction. Each train had a gripper to hold the cable, and when it entered a station the driver released the gripper and coasted to a halt. Power for the cable was supplied by massive stationary engines, which kept the cables moving at a steady 20 km/h, the speed of the trains.

Tunnelling under the Clyde was a problem. To keep water out of the tunnels, the air pressure inside the tunnel had to be very high, so that it forced water out of the workings. At one freak low tide in 1894, there was so little water in the river above the tunnel that there was an explosion. Timber and metal shot up from the tunnel into the river, and floated away or sank.

The Subway, as Glaswegians call it, opened in 1896. Cable haulage was in use until 1934, when it was replaced by electricity. The rolling stock was made to last eighty years!

Cable haulage on the Blackwall Railway. Notice the huge cable drums at the end of the line

Glasgow's original carriages, in use for over 80 years

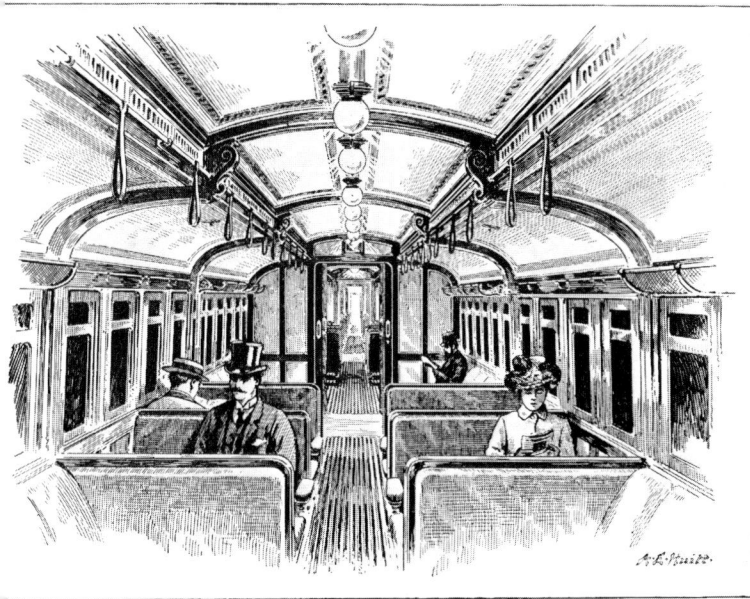

The interior design of carriages on the 'twopenny tube' was a great advance on the City & South London. Notice the straps for standing passengers

Bank Station, 1903

The twopenny tube

The great success of the City & South London Railway encouraged companies to build more deep level lines. The next major 'tube' line was the Central, opened in 1900.

It was lighter and airier than the earlier tube, with larger tunnels and stations, electric lifts and electric lighting in the station instead of gas. The tunnels were planned so that the platforms were on a hump. Incoming trains were slowed down, whilst outgoing trains could accelerate rapidly downhill.

But the new idea which proved really popular was the standard fare. Passengers paid twopence to travel any distance along the line. The Central Railway was its official name, but it was always known as 'the twopenny tube'.

On a single day in its first summer of working, the twopenny tube carried a quarter of a million passengers. The success of this tube was immediately followed by yet more deep-level lines, and by the electrification of the older Metropolitan and District Railways.

The first trains on the line had separate locomotives, but these were badly designed and set up vibrations. Buildings above the line were shaken. So the locomotives were replaced by motor-coaches and trailers, like this 1903 stock

District line stock, 1905. Notice the sliding doors instead of gates

8 Roads without Horses

Trams

Because horse trams were slow, experiments were made with steam-power on a few routes in the 1880s, in Glasgow, Huddersfield, Lancashire, parts of the Midlands and on one route in London. Normal steam locomotives would have been dangerous as well as noisy and filthy, so steam trams were built with no moving parts on the outside, such as pistons and driving wheels, which could have hurt people or horses.

The locomotive might have some seats for passengers, but most people preferred to travel in the trailer car.

Compressed air tram, with trailer, 1884

Steam trams, each with two trailers, in Sydney, Australia, 1889

Cable trams in San Francisco were very successful on the steep hills

Steam trams were unpopular, but experiments were being made all over the world to replace horses. Cable haulage was successful in San Francisco, Chicago, Melbourne (where it was in use from 1885 to 1940) and elsewhere. Compressed air, naphtha engines and even gas were all tried in the 1880s with slight success.

The ideal motive power for tramways turned out to be electricity.

The first public electric tramway opened near Berlin in 1881. It was unsafe because it used the running rails to provide current, and anyone who touched the rails could be killed.

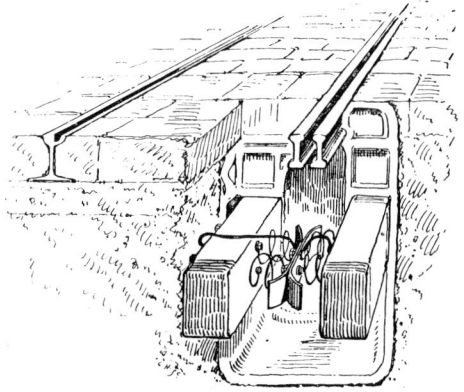

An experiment with electric traction at Northfleet, Kent, in 1889. The cut-away drawing shows how it worked. A 'plough' inside one of the running rails pushed between the contact points, which are on springs

Improved versions mostly used a 'plough' which ran in a slot in the road and collected current from a conductor rail hidden below the surface, or else they collected the current from overhead wires.

One alternative was a row of studs in the road, which carried the current. Under the tram was a 'skate' with an electromagnet which pulled the stud up into contact with the skate.

The skate and stud system in use at Wolverhampton. The close-up photograph shows what the studs looked like

The Bessbrook & Newry tramway, 1885. Notice how on this cross-country route the tram is towing ordinary railway trucks. The tramway carried goods as well as passengers

Many experimental electric lines were opened in the 1880s. Two of the most successful were in Ireland—the Giant's Causeway Railway (1883) and the Bessbrook & Newry (1885). Both ran through the country, however, not in towns.

In England the first overhead trolley tramway was at Roundhay, Leeds, in 1891, and by 1900 almost all the industrial cities of Britain had electric tramways, except London.

London rapidly caught up, once electrification came in, with over 500 km of electric routes built between 1901 and 1914. There were three private companies and a number of local authorities, especially in East London.

Between 1895 and 1914, 105 local authorities in Britain and 74 private companies started tramway systems. Most of the systems had their own power station, because they preferred 'direct current' to the mains supply of 'alternating current'. There was not much co-operation between all these systems, which made it difficult later on when the time came to join the small systems together.

One of Liverpool's first electric trams

Roundhay, Leeds—the first overhead trolley tramway in England, opened in 1891

Municipal celebrations often greeted the first trams. These are in Ealing

Below: Boar Lane, Leeds, in 1921. The driver here does have a windscreen

Tram design

In the early 1900s, top deck passengers travelled out in the open. Roofs were put on most trams from about 1911. The driver's cab was not enclosed because of the danger from broken glass if there was a collision, but even after safety glass was invented, some drivers were left exposed to rain, frost or snow.

If you want to study the way trams developed, from the single decker horse tram of the 1870s until 1953, when the last tram was built in Britain, the best place to do so is at the Tramway Museum at Crich, near Matlock. There, on summer weekends, you can actually travel on different types of tram, as well as walking round the tram sheds which contain over 40 trams.

Steam bus, 1902

Experimental petrol/electric bus, 1903. It was never put into service

Motor bus, 1901

Drivers at Cricklewood Garage, ready for the day's work

Buses

The first people to try out a new invention often lose a lot of money, and the people who follow can profit by learning from the early mistakes. This certainly happened with horseless buses.

A battery-powered bus was tried in 1897 and a petrol engined one in 1897, but all the stopping and starting in traffic was too much for them.

Tyres were a problem with all early motor cars, but especially with buses. Pneumatic tyres were very costly. They lasted at best for 2000 km, and they could not support a heavy vehicle. Passengers did not like stopping while a tyre was changed.

Solid tyres were used for heavier buses but they tended to disintegrate, or even to fly off the wheel and bound along the road. One bus operator said that tyres alone cost him ten pence per mile, at a time when a tram cost only a shilling (twelve pence) a mile including the crew's wages. The drivers were new to the job, and passengers complained of their jerky driving. A number of the early operators despaired and gave up their efforts.

Then came a sudden breakthrough. By 1905 it was possible to control the throttle. Before that, the power was either on or off, and the gears were used to control the speed. Better tyres could now be bought. In 1910 the London General Omnibus Company introduced the 34-seater 'B-type', which was so good a design that nearly 3000 were built.

Motor buses dominate the traffic, London 1912

By 1912 horse buses cost 1/3d a mile to operate, trams 1/- and motor buses just 7d. Yet by that time the electric tramways had such a hold, that very few cities in Britain, except London, had many buses.

One great handicap of trams compared with buses was that the tram companies had to maintain the roadway on either side of their tracks. This was covered by a law, the Tramway Act. It was rather unfair, because trams running on tracks did not wear out the road, except by some vibration.

Buses, on the other hand, which *did* wear out the roads, did not have to pay much towards road repairs. Transport experts who favour trams and railways have always been bitter about this kind of 'subsidy' to road transport.

At the wheel of a B-type. Notice the gear and hand brake mechanisms on the outside of the bus

London Road-Car Company bus, 1909, with a flagpole over the cab

An electric cab

Liverpool's first taxi, 1906. The bonnet has a flap for air-cooling. Just above the steering-wheel you can see the taximeter clock itself. You could travel 1½ miles for a shilling (5p)

The motor taxi

Electric cabs, like electric buses, were tried and were a failure during the 1890s. Tyres were a nuisance, batteries weighed as much as two tons and wore out quickly. Moreover, these 'humming bird' cabs were outpaced by hansoms.

Vauxhall produced a motorised hansom, with the driver on an outrigger at the back just like the horse-drawn version, but it was never used.

When motor taxis did suceed, about 1908, they were regarded as 'horrid motors'. They were only used because, unlike hansoms, they had meters to show the distance travelled. Londoners had been cheated by cabbies for long enough. By 1909 you could buy a second-hand hansom for just £1 !

Edwardian taxis were brightly painted in the livery of the owners—orange with black lines, all white, grey with a yellow bonnet. They were used by the well-to-do for shopping, by business people in a hurry, and by train travellers crossing London from one terminus to another.

Taxicabs passing a canvas-hooded bus, 1923

The Metropolitan Police laid down dimensions for taxis. As a result, a special vehicle was developed—high off the ground, very comfortable, with an amazing turning circle, but rather slow.

Other cities have preferred to use ordinary cars, often painted a special colour, for example bright yellow in New York. In some cities, yellow painted taxis have taxi-meters, and other taxis do not—so unless you use a yellow taxi you may be cheated.

London taxi-drivers have to pass a thorough test both of their driving skill and of 'the Knowledge'. This means knowing street names, basic routes, the names of hotels and institutions. It takes over a year to learn, during which the candidate (called a 'butter-boy') travels round on a scooter. Three out of four candidates fail the exam.

Taxi at the Savoy, 1904. Underneath you can just see the chain drive from the engine to the back wheels

Public ownership

The first bus services, urban railways and tramways were all privately owned. The first exception was when Huddersfield, in 1883, found that nobody wanted to operate the new tramway they had planned. So the Council decided to operate it themselves.

The Tramway Act of 1870 allowed local authorities to buy the tramways in their area, and many did. They saw that tramways helped local people, and also the shopkeepers, whose customers arrived by tram.

Probably very few tramways were ever profitable to run. Certainly suburban train services never were, even when they were privately owned. Too many people want to travel in the rush hours, which means that a lot of rolling stock is needed—but this is *only* used in the rush hours. To make a profit, less rolling stock needs to be in use almost all the time.

The private transport companies had made their profit out of rising land values, as explained on page 22. Once the land was built up, the companies withdrew the loss-making services—and the local authority was left to provide some kind of transport for the area.

Shepherd's Bush, Whit Monday, 1903. Not one private carriage is in sight

Notice the safety gate under the front of the tram. If a pedestrian fell, this gadget would catch him

So many men went to fight in 1914 that women began to be employed as conductresses and drivers on trams. These are in Glasgow. Many motor buses were taken to France to carry troops

9 Between the Wars

Many privately owned railways and tramways, and even bus services, went bankrupt. Small companies were taken over by large ones. The whole transport of great cities became the monopoly of one or two huge firms.

London had just one large bus company, two large tram companies (which did not run competing routes) and an 'Underground group'—a vast company which controlled both the tram companies. Many tram routes were already run by local authorities.

Once a single firm controlled so much, it seemed too powerful to be left in private hands. The solution chosen in 1933 was to create a publicly owned Board, later called London Transport, directed by the London County Council.

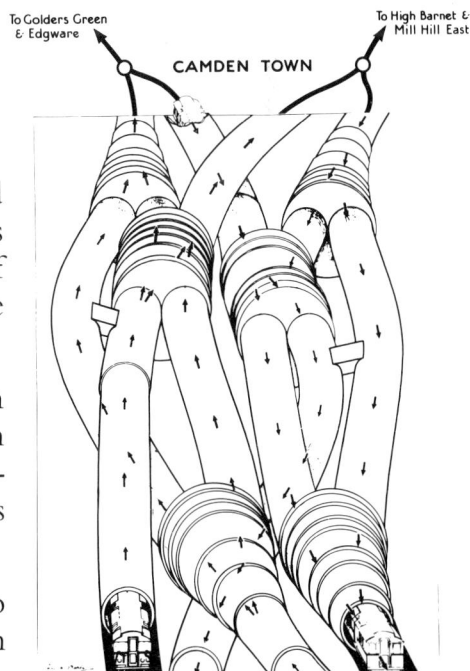

Many tube lines were extended in the 1920s. This is a complex Northern Line junction

Euston & Hampstead (later Northern) Line, 1920 stock, inside and outside

Hampstead & City (later Northern) Line, 1923 stock, inside and outside

How tube train design changed between 1920 and 1969, when the Victoria Line stock (right) came into use

London Transport was able to reorganise the various systems to cooperate with each other. Like transport systems in practically all the major cities of the world, it has to be subsidised by public money.

Tram tracks were usually laid in the middle of the road. Cars were supposed to stop while passengers boarded the trams. As you can see here, the motorists did not always wait, pedestrians wandered about the road and buses added to the confusion

The motor car

Before 1914, the various forms of public transport—bus, tram, underground, suburban railway—were all competing against each other. Gradually this changed. Nowadays all public transport is competing against private transport—the car.

Between the wars, commuters began to use cars to drive to work. It meant they didn't have to look at a timetable before travelling and they didn't get wet waiting at a bus stop or on a platform. Above all, they were seen to be a well-off and important person, who could afford to run a car. They could also live away from transport routes, and even right outside the cities.

New tram designs, such as this Feltham class, were made in the 1930s, but not many new trams were built. The old stock became rather shabby

The catalogue of an early Motor Show. From the first, car manufacturers appealed to snobbery

But city streets were busy, and traffic jams were a nuisance. Some other types of vehicles were particularly troublesome in the eyes of the motorist. Horse-drawn vehicles were slow, but there were fewer of them each year. Trams were the worst.

The tram tracks were laid in the middle of the road. When the tram stopped, the motorist was not allowed to overtake on the inside. He had to wait until all the passengers had boarded the tram.

When there were no trams in sight, the tracks were still dangerous. A narrow car tyre could get stuck in the groove and cause an accident, unless the driver took care.

A full tramcar carried 80–90 passengers while most commuter cars carry only the driver. It was not unfair that the trams had priority, but motorists still became impatient.

Because important decisions about transport were bound to be taken by important kinds of people, who came to their work by car and not on a twopenny tram ticket, the attitude of the motorists mattered a great deal.

Tram versus bus

From the 1920s on, the people who ran local transport had to decide whether to carry on with trams or switch to buses. From 1925, tramway systems began to disappear one by one, until now in Britain there are none left at all, except as tourist attractions.

Yet in many other countries in Europe, and in Canada, modernised trams are a successful form of city transport. Why did the bus win in Britain?

Cartoon of 1913

1925 double-decker: the staircase is still open

B-type bus, designed about 1910, in use here in 1920. Compare it with the later double-deckers shown on the left

This 1949 design, built for routes with low bridges, looks almost like a modern bus

Birmingham, 1957

London, 1943

For the bus:

1 Trams slowed down other road traffic.
2 Tramcars lasted a long time—as much as 60 years, compared to 12–15 years for a bus. This is really in favour of the tram, but it meant that many old tramcars were always in use. When times were hard, and in wartime, trams were not modernised. Buses *had* to be replaced, because they fell to bits, so buses seemed a 'more modern form of transport'.
3 It was easy to alter a bus route, but tram tracks were a fixture.
4 If a tram broke down, it blocked the line until it was pushed away.
5 Private tramways still had to maintain the roadway. Tramway companies changed to buses much sooner than local authorities who ran trams.
6 The petrol companies and the motor manufacturers have always been very powerful in politics. They pressed hard for buses.

For the tram:

1 Trams carried more passengers. The Swansea & Mumbles trams seated 106, so, with two cars coupled, a crew of three (one driver, two conductors) carried 212 seated passengers. Trams did not overturn, no matter how many passengers were carried standing.
2 Tram fares were cheaper.
3 Trams could run even in thick fog and smog, which used to be common in smoky cities. They could also carry snowploughs, saving the council from keeping them.
4 Trams were safer than buses.
5 They were much cleaner than diesel or petrol buses.

The greatest advantage of trams nowadays would be that they run on electricity, which can be made from coal, gas, oil, nuclear energy, or whatever other fuel may be cheapest. Buses are dependent on oil, which at the moment is expensive.

The trolleybus

Many tramways were replaced by trolleybuses. These took current from the overhead wires which the trams had used but they did not need tracks.

The pioneering local authorities were Leeds and Bradford, starting routes in 1911, but it was in Teesside that the vehicle really developed. Early trolleybuses were heavy, trackless trams, but in 1922 Teesside began using converted petrol buses.

Trolleybuses had all the advantages of electric power, such as cleanness, swift acceleration and braking, and the use of existing electric generators.

From about 1950 the number of passengers has been falling. Trolleybuses, like trams, had heavy 'fixed costs'. The overhead wires had to be maintained just the same, even if only half the number of vehicles were used. So, as more passengers became car owners, the trolleybuses became less economic. Now there are none left.

An early American design for a trolleybus

York trolleybus, 1912

Trolleybuses are efficient at moving large numbers of people. These are moving a 1930s football crowd in Tottenham

Pedestrians thread their way through jammed traffic

10 Public Transport Now

Now that we have so many cars, do we need public transport at all? Not everyone has a car—old people, people too young to have a licence or too poor to own a car, wives whose husbands drive the family car to work, all these people have no access to a car. And even the motorist sometimes needs public transport.

So public transport is needed by all of us some of the time, and by some of us all of the time. For years vast sums of money have been spent on making better roads. But better roads actually attract car drivers who before went by public transport.

As the buses carry fewer people, and the traffic gets thicker, the bus operator loses money faster and has to reduce the number of buses. So passengers will spend longer at the bus stop and yet more people turn to cars.

Transport planners, who work for the government and the local authorities, now see this 'vicious circle' and are at last trying to reverse it—though they may not succeed. The idea is that if buses or trains were better, more people would use them. That would produce more income, so that another round of improvements could be made.

Birmingham 1954. The city later made most of the main roads in its centre into dual carriageways. Would that be a good solution in York, which has many historic buildings?

In Los Angeles, California, there is very little public transport. Everyone needs a car. Large parts of the land area are devoted to motorway interchanges

The car has brought much greater freedom of choice to car-owners. With a car you can go where you want, when you want, provided that not too many car drivers want to do the same thing. The disadvantages of car use fall mainly on other people than the driver: they include noise, thicker traffic, worse public transport and polluted air.

The key to making people use buses and trains would probably be to make public transport so cheap, so fast and so comfortable that people actually prefer to use it. An attempt to reduce prices was made in London in 1983, but it was said to be against the law for the Council to give a big subsidy to London Transport.

Car drivers can no longer expect the consideration they have had in recent years—with buildings knocked down for improved one-way systems, and pedestrians forced through sewer-like underpasses or over uncovered footbridges in a city planned for cars.

Motorists will find fewer and more expensive parking places in years to come, as the planners deliberately try to stop commuters from using cars. Motorists may even need a special licence to enter city centres.

Separating pedestrians and wheeled traffic was just a joke in 1900

Pedestrians

City centres are places for people to meet each other, and also to shop. Some cities have banned all vehicles from the older central shopping streets, and some allow only buses, taxis and delivery vans. The result is that people feel safer, they seem more friendly, they are prouder of their city.

These converted 'shopping precincts' seem to be more successful than ones which are purpose-built. The older streets have been given back their original use.

Where people are collecting heavy shopping at a supermarket, it is usually possible to arrange car parking at the back of the store, especially in new precincts. Delivery lorries also need to be able to unload.

Cyclists

Cycling is coming back into fashion, though it is most unlikely that the majority of people will take up cycling. Some cities provide special bike routes. This has been done in Stevenage and other sprawling new towns, which seem to have been designed for motorists or people content to stay at home.

In these towns the pedestrian has too far to walk from his 'neighbourhood' to the town centre shops, so he has to rely on the buses or taxis.

Pedestrian precinct in Leeds

The kind of main road which takes traffic around a pedestrian area. This is Mancunian Way in Manchester. Compare it with the railway on page 26

The bus with a phone number—a London Transport experiment now abandoned

Smaller buses and new systems

When a town's population is spread out, as in many suburbs and new towns, there are not enough people in an area to keep normal buses running, except at a loss. One solution, tried first in America and now in Britain, is to use a minibus.

The minibus carries about 20 people. Although the driver has a set route, he is prepared to go a short distance off it, if asked. The fares are slightly higher than on ordinary buses, but women with shopping and young children are happy to pay for the extra convenience. Experiments have been made with 'dial-a-ride' services, where passengers could phone for the bus to come to their door.

A strange experiment was tried in a Toronto suburb. Regular commuters, who wanted to use a bus but lived too far from a bus stop, were taken by taxi to meet the bus. The bus company subsidised the taxi company, so the taxi fare was just 10 cents (5p). The total state subsidy needed was *less* than was needed before for the bus service alone.

The Leyland 'minibus' is used in residential areas where there is no regular service and on normal bus routes where roads don't permit larger vehicles

Other bus experiments

Bus lanes and 'buses only' streets are kept free for buses so that they don't get caught in jams. A rush-hour bus carries 80 people, so it rightly has priority over cars which mostly carry one. Bus lanes also allow buses to drive with blazing headlights down one-way streets against the flow of traffic, saving journey time.

Traffic lights can be programmed to change to green as a bus approaches.

Fixed fares and one-man crews are not popular with passengers. The conductor's wages are saved, but the bus waits at each stop as the passengers board. Some bus operators are experimenting with the French and German system of buying the ticket (or several tickets at once) in advance at a slot machine.

Newly designed buses carry more passengers by providing fewer seats and more standing room. Separate exits and entrances make stops shorter.

Pay-as-you-enter bus, 1970s

The 90-seater Leyland Olympian, 1982

Pay-as-you-enter and exact fares are not a new idea. This is a London United Tramways tram in 1922

The 'Silent Rider' in Manchester, 1975

A familiar electric vehicle, the milk-float

New sources of power for buses

Experiments have been made with single-deck battery-powered buses. The 'Silent Rider' in Manchester travelled 65 km on a single charge of the battery, which was enough to last through the morning rush hour. The battery was recharged over lunch. There may be improved batteries in the future, and they might be interchangeable, but their development has been disappointingly slow.

Trolleybuses may also be revived, but with one important difference. If they could sometimes leave the wires, say for 10 km, and then return to a further length of wire, routes could be more easily changed and much less overhead gear would need to be expensively maintained.

The answer here may be flywheel power. A large flywheel is run up to high speed by an electric motor, and then its energy is gradually drawn off to keep the bus moving. A Swiss flywheel bus was in use in Kinshasa, Zaire, between 1953 and 1969. Much better flywheels are made now than that bus used.

Ford's first experimental electric city car, The Comuta, built in the 1960s

The 820 m Byker viaduct carries the new metro line over the Ouseburn valley

Glasgow tram on reserved track at Knightswood. If there had been more reserved track, the trams might never have been scrapped. The last Glasgow tram ran in 1962

Inside the station tunnel at Heathrow Airport, in 1974

Rapid-transit systems

'Rapid-transit' is just a name given to all inner-city railways, whether underground, elevated or surface, including some which are more like high-speed trams than main-line trains.

The new Newcastle and Gateshead Metro is served by 168-seater trams, running between unmanned stations, partly underground, but mostly on old British Rail routes.

These modern trams can reach 80 km/h very quickly. Good acceleration and braking matter far more than top speed.

Good connections with buses, and car parks at stations, encourage more people to use the new system.

London's underground system is still expanding. The Victoria Line, which could operate fully automatically, was a success, and extensions to London Airport and to the Jubilee Line between Baker Street and Charing Cross have been made.

Unfortunately on the London Underground the trains stop at every station. New sets of express lines, running parallel to the existing routes, are badly needed.

If passengers are to be attracted from cars to rapid-transit, comfort is needed as well as speed. In Montreal, Canada, and Paris there are underground trains with pneumatic tyres running on concrete rails, which makes for a smoother ride. The trains are guided by horizontal wheels running against metal rails.

San Francisco has a new system designed specially to attract commuters away from their cars. Comfortable seats, fitted carpets, air-conditioning and no room at all for standing passengers are combined with high speeds. Since the train timing has to be accurate to within five seconds, the whole running of the system is done by a computer, which even shuts the carriage doors.

This diagram of an important interchange station on the London Underground shows why building new lines is so expensive

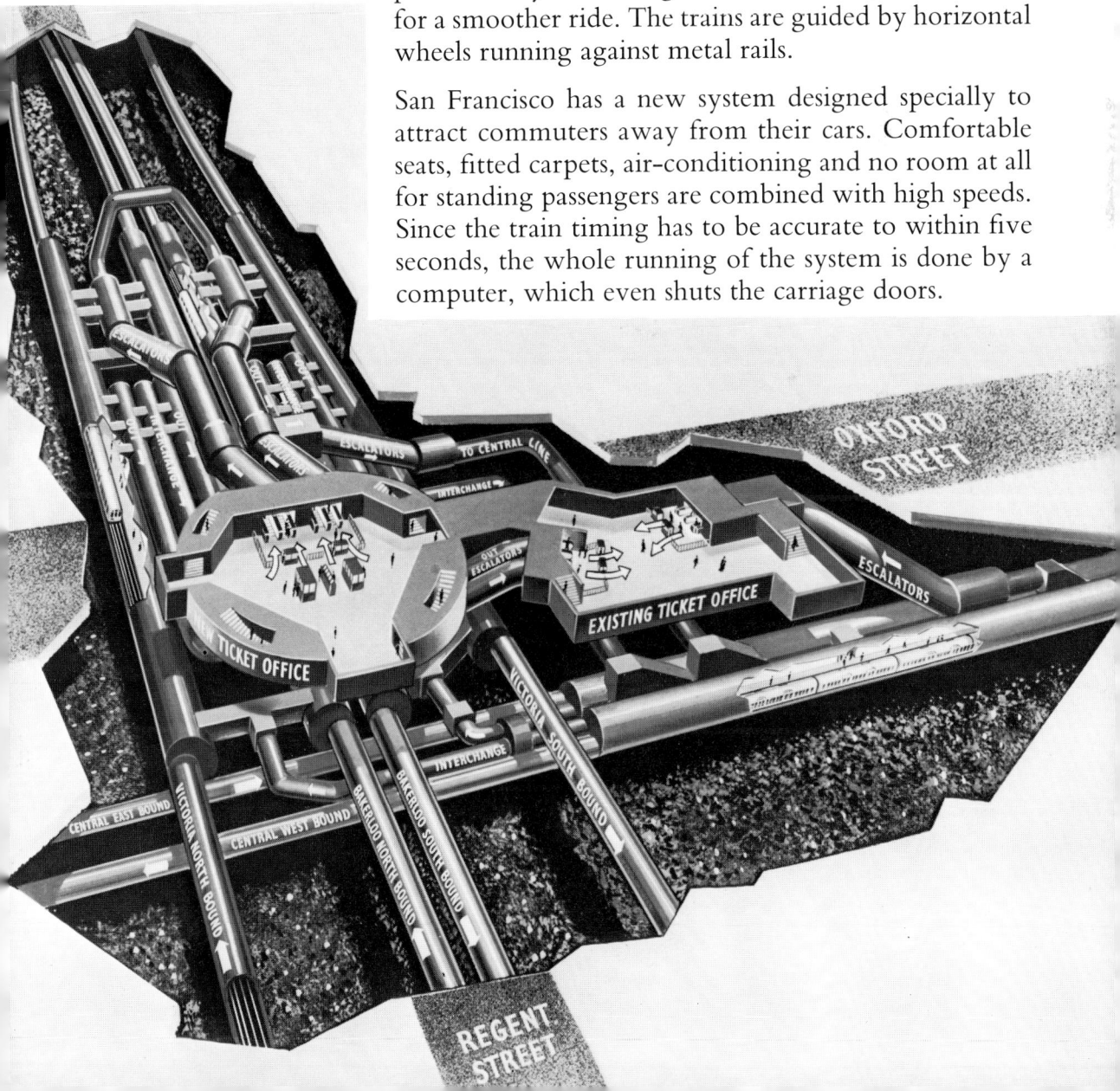

An idea put forward about 1900, but never tried. The carriages slow down to less than walking pace as they enter a station, but never quite stop

Getting about in city rush hours is something everybody hates. If going by public transport was more comfortable and didn't involve strap-hanging in airless, smelly, rattling carriages, or queuing to get onto an escalator, commuters would be happy to use public transport.

And that in its turn would mean fewer cars, and streets freer for buses and essential vehicles. Above all, our cities could be pleasanter places to live and work.

Because our present public transport is already overcrowded, it seems an impossible dream to want it to carry more people and be more comfortable. It would certainly mean that the government would have to spend the money needed for new and better services as well as paying towards running costs.

If the money is not spent, there is a serious chance that public transport could stop entirely. No-one knows what would happen then.

An articulated lorry taking a difficult corner in Chepstow. It is going onto the kerb, and could easily run over a pedestrian on the footpath

Some points to discuss

Through traffic

1 Does your town or city suffer from traffic on major roads which pass through the town? If you have a by-pass or ring road, when was it built? Does it work well now?

2 Would it help to ban 'juggernaut' lorries from town centres? Could this be done, and what effects would it have?

3 Why does so much freight go by road and not by rail? Can you discover what is meant by double-handling, and why it is so expensive?

4 Many plans for new roads have been scrapped since 1970. Were there plans for new roads in your town? If so, where exactly would they have gone? What buildings or open land would they have replaced? What arguments did people use for or against the new road?

An improved interchange between surface railway, underground and bus station. Until the 1970s bus passengers had to wait in the open: now they have some protection

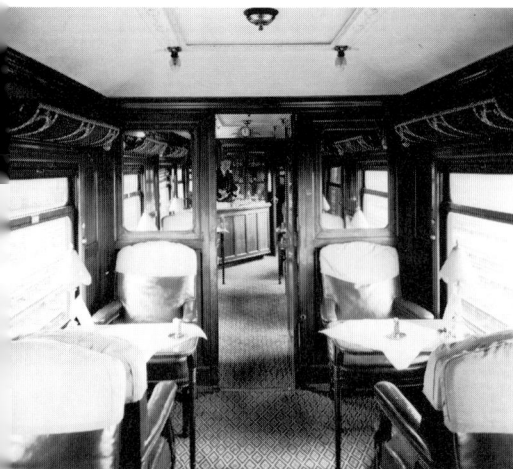

Luxury travel on a suburban train in 1934—modern commuters do not expect this amount of comfort!

Commuters

5 If you know people who travel to work every day, you could ask them about their journey. How do they travel? Have they tried other ways of making the journey? What is difficult or irritating about it? Would better 'interchanges' help? If they have to wait for a train or bus, do they have to stand out in the cold during the winter or can they sit in a comfortable waiting room?

6 Some cities have built large free car parks at stations or bus stops on the outskirts of a city, to encourage people to 'park-and-ride'. Would this attract more people to public transport in your town? If so, would the same car park serve the needs of both commuters and shoppers?

7 You could do a survey of the number of cars on a main road into your city during rush hours, and again during shopping hours. What is the average number of people in each car? Compare it with the average in a bus at the same time. Your survey would be particularly interesting at a road junction, but you would need a team of people working with you. Can you think of a way of showing in a diagram the number of vehicles (or the total number of people) going in each direction?

8 What ways can you think of to attract people back to public transport?

9 Some transport planners now think it will be impossible to attract car-drivers back to public transport. They say it will be necessary to 'restrain' motorists from entering city-centres without a really good reason. How could they do this—and is it a good idea?

Shopping centres

10 There was no space in this book to discuss vans which deliver goods to shops. Do these vans block traffic in your town? What could be done about it? (You might ask both van drivers and shoppers what they think.)

11 Are high streets and town centres necessary? Could they be replaced by massive shopping centres or hypermarkets in the outskirts?

12 Would it help your town centre if pedestrians and cars were more separated? Who would gain and who would lose?

Book list

Books marked ★ are more difficult. They are worth looking at for detail, or if you want to study the subject more deeply.

General

Roads and Vehicles,★ Anthony Bird, Longman
The Midlands: Towns & Cities, Clive Gilbert, Wayland
The Great Transport Game, Julian Cummins, ILEA Media Resources Centre
Instead of Cars,★ Terence Bendixon, Temple Smith
Access for All,★ K H Schaeffer & Eliot Sclar, Penguin
Semi-detached London,★ Alan A Jackson, Allen & Unwin
Diary of a Nobody, G & W Grossmith, Dent or Collins

Underground Railways

Underground Railways of the World, O S Nock, Black (out of print)
The Story of London's Underground, John R Day, London Transport

Buses

Discovering Old Buses and Trolleybuses, David Kaye, Shire
Buses and Trolleybuses before 1919, David Kaye, Blandford
Buses and Trolleybuses 1919–1945, David Kaye, Blandford
Buses, Trolleybuses and Trams, Chas. S Dunbar, Hamlyn
The Story of the London Bus, John R Day, London Transport

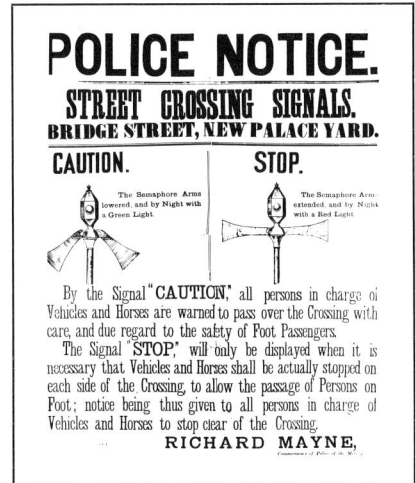

An announcement of the first traffic lights

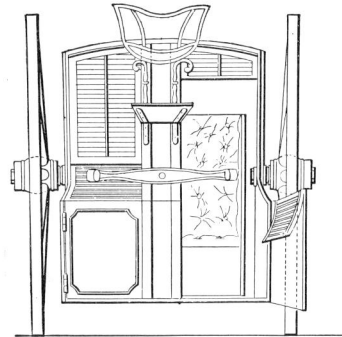

Joseph Hansom's original design of 1834. Notice the huge wheels, and the driver's seat placed over the shafts

Index